NATIONAL
GEOGRAPHIC

Baking Bread

Faridah Yusof

Dad

bowl

ear

2

I **hear** Dad.
I hear Dad mixing things in a bowl.
I **hear** with my ears.

oven

Dad

pan

4

I **see** Dad.

I see Dad put a pan in the oven.

I **see** with my eyes.

nose

bread

6

I **smell** the bread.
It smells great.
I **smell** with my nose.

hand

bread

8

I **touch** the bread.

It is warm.

I **touch** with my hands.

bread

I **taste** the bread.
It is good.
I **taste** with my tongue.

Yum!